QUOTING 2018

SHANNA STAR

DIVINE CREATIVE, LLC. ™

Printed in the United States of America

First Printing, 2021

ISBN 9-7985947439-8-4

www.amazon.com/author/shannastar

COVER CREDIT:

PHOTO TAKEN BY: ISAAC MADERA

KYLE & SHANNA 2016

DEDICATIONS

TO MY SON, EVERY WAKING MINUTE, LOVE IS SENT TO YOU, WITH A PRAYER THAT CLARITY BE CAST UPON YOU, OF THE TRUTHS OF WHO I AM, AND WHO YOU ARE. MAY THOSE WHO LIE AND MANIPULATE YOUR MIND, BE REVEALED TO YOU. I LOVE YOU BABY BOY.

LOVE, MOM

TO KYLE, THANK YOU FOR AWAKENING MY SOUL. THANK YOU FOR BEING A PART OF MULTIPLE STEPS ON MY PATH, AND THANK YOU FOR GIVING YOUR LIFE, SO THAT I MAY SERVE MINE. THANK YOU FOR JOINING ME IN MY JOURNEY FROM A HIGHER LEVEL. I LOVE YOU.

"

THINK OF ME AS THE OCEAN. MY DEPTHS AREN'T MEANT TO BE FULLY DISCOVERED OR UNDERSTOOD. INSTEAD OF TRYING TO UNCOVER THESE DEPTHS, ALLOW ME TO REVEAL THEM, IN THEIR OWN TIMING, IN WAVES WITH A NATURAL FLOW, FOR THE EVOLUTION OF HUMANITY.

"

IF YOU WANT THE CHANCE TO SHOW PEOPLE,
YOU'RE BETTER THAN YOUR PAST, YOU MUST
GIVE PEOPLE A CHANCE TO ALSO BE BETTER
THAN THEIR PAST.

A THERAPIST CANNOT HELP YOU REMEMBER
WHO YOU ARE, ONLY THE INTERNAL WORK
BETWEEN YOU AND THE UNIVERSE / GOD /
YOUR HIGHER SELF, CAN DO THAT.

ACKNOWLEDGMENT OF YOUR PERSONAL
TRUTHS WILL BRING CLARITY TO YOUR PATH.

"

WHEN YOU START CHANGING THE WAY YOU ADDRESS THE CIRCUMSTANCES IN YOUR LIFE, THE CIRCUMSTANCES IN YOUR LIFE START TO CHANGE.

BOUNDARIES CAN BE SET, CORDS CAN BE CUT, BUT YOU STILL MUST ALLOW TIME. YOU DIDN'T DEVELOP LOVE FOR A PERSON OVERNIGHT, DON'T EXPECT TO 'UNFEEL' OVERNIGHT. BE PATIENT WITH YOURSELF.

IT'S IMPORTANT TO RELEASE THE NEED FOR LOGIC OR AN EXPLANATION, AND ALLOW YOURSELF TO 'JUST BE' BECAUSE IT IS IN THE ACT OF JUST BEING, THAT YOU ALLOW YOURSELF TO RECEIVE THE REAL ANSWERS IN LIFE.

"

ADMITTING TO MYSELF HOW MUCH I LIED TO MYSELF, ABOUT MYSELF, WAS DISAPPOINTING WHEN REALIZED. WE WOULD HATE TO THINK THAT WE AREN'T AS GOOD OF A PERSON, AS WE MAKE OURSELVES LOOK. EVEN THOUGH #PEOPLELIKEUS HAVE A HUGE HEART WITH PURE INTENTIONS, AND GENUINE LOVE TO GIVE, WE ALSO HAVE CONS TO OUR PROS. UNTIL YOU CAN LET YOUR PRIDE DOWN TO ACKNOWLEDGE YOUR CONS, YOU WILL BE STUCK IN THE DELUSION THAT YOU DON'T HAVE ANY, OR THAT THEY'RE REALLY NOT THAT BAD. BEING HONEST WITH YOURSELF IS ESSENTIAL IN ENDING THE CYCLES YOU KEEP REPEATING IN LIFE. HONESTY WITH YOURSELF WILL BRING ABOUT THE DEATH OF EVERYTHING YOU THINK YOU ARE ALLOWING YOU TO TRANSITION INTO THE REBIRTH OF EVERYTHING YOU REALLY ARE. MAKE THE DECISION TO BE HONEST WITH YOURSELF SO THAT YOU CAN LOVE YOURSELF. THANK YOU TASHA, FOR OPENING THE FLOOD GATES FOR ME.

"

THERE ARE ANGELS IN HUMAN FORM SENT
HERE TO HELP YOU. BE CAREFUL WHO YOU PUSH
AWAY.

WHEN OTHERS TRIGGER ANY PARTICULAR
FEELING IN YOU, ANGER, SADNESS, ETC., THEY
ARE BEING USED TO SHOW YOU WHAT IS
UNHEALED INSIDE OF YOURSELF.

ANSWERS CANNOT COME TO A MIND AT FULL
CAPACITY.

"

DON'T EXPECT TO ATTRACT HONEST PEOPLE,
UNTIL YOU, YOURSELF, ARE HONEST.

ALLOW YOURSELF TO BE WHO YOU ARE.

WHEN YOU SEE BEAUTY IN THE WORLD, TREES,
ANIMALS, SKY, AND OCEANS, REMEMBER THAT
SAME BEAUTY RESIDES IN YOU. WE ARE ALL ONE,
ALWAYS HAVE BEEN, ALWAYS WILL BE.

BEFORE GETTING OFFENDED, FIRST ASK
YOURSELF, IS WHAT'S OFFENDING YOU TRUE?
AND BE HONEST IN YOUR ANSWER.

"

BEFORE SPEAKING NEGATIVELY ABOUT ANOTHER, REMEMBER THE THINGS YOU HAVE DONE, THAT ARE LESS APPEALING. YOUR JUDGMENT SHOULD THEN BE REPLACED WITH HUMILITY.

THE BEST VERSION OF YOURSELF RESTS IN THE HANDS OF HONESTY, INCLUDING BEING HONEST WITH YOURSELF WHEN YOU KNOW SOMEONE ISN'T GOOD FOR YOUR LIFE.

GROWTH WILL NEVER OCCUR IF YOU CONTINUE TO BLAME OBSTACLES ON THE 'DEVIL TESTING YOU' .. IT IS THE UNIVERSE TRYING TO TEACH YOU A LESSON ABOUT YOURSELF. THE TEST IS, WILL YOU LEARN THE LESSON?

"

WHEN A PERSON BRINGS OUT THE WORST IN YOU, IT IS TRULY THEM SHOWING YOU WHAT ALREADY RESIDES WITHIN.

BY LOVING OURSELVES, WE SHOW OTHERS OUR WORTH.

YOU CANNOT ASK ONE TO GROW, THEN PLACE THEM IN A BOX, IN FEAR OF THEM GROWING DIFFERENTLY THAN YOU EXPECTED THEM TO.

"

YOU CANNOT HELP A PERSON SEE IN THE DARK,
IF THEY REFUSE TO REMOVE THEIR SHADES.
MOVE FORWARD.

YOU CANNOT HOLD ANOTHER TO CERTAIN
EXPECTATIONS THEY KNOW NOTHING ABOUT,
AND BE UPSET WHEN THEY DON'T MEET THOSE
EXPECTATIONS.

YOU CANNOT BLAME THE PASSENGER IF YOU HIT
A TREE WHILE DRIVING. YOU ARE THE DRIVER
OF YOUR LIFE, AND YOU CHOOSE THE
PASSENGERS.

"

YOUR CAREER DOES NOT DEFINE YOU; IT
MERELY DEFINES HOW YOU'VE BEEN TAUGHT TO
SUPPORT YOURSELF.

CHANGE IS THE ONLY GUARANTEED
OCCURRENCE IN LIFE THAT WILL
CONTINUOUSLY TAKE YOU TO NEW LEVELS.
DEPENDING ON THE DECISIONS YOU MAKE,
THOSE LEVELS CAN ALWAYS BE HIGHER AND
BETTER THAN THE LAST.

CHANGE WILL NOT OCCUR BY COMPLAINING
ABOUT THE PROBLEM, BUT BY TAKING ACTION
TO RESOLVE THE PROBLEM.

"

WHILE CHECKING ON EVERYONE ELSE, DON'T FORGET TO TEND TO YOUR OWN WELL-BEING, THAT IS THE MOST IMPORTANT.

THERE'S NOTHING WRONG WITH YOU CHOOSING YOU.

IN CHOOSING SILENCE WHILE ANOTHER WANTS TO ARGUE OR ACT IN A FIT OF RAGE, YOU ARE DEMONSTRATING STRENGTH AND PEACE WITHIN YOURSELF.

"

CLARITY WILL ONLY BE GAINED SECONDARY TO
THE PRESENCE OF HONESTY.

THERE IS COMPASSION TO BE FOUND FOR
EVERY PERSON YOU ENCOUNTER, BY
UNDERSTANDING THAT JUST LIKE YOU, THEY
ARE BROKEN ON THE INSIDE.

WHEN CONFUSION SETS IN, BRING YOURSELF
BACK TO THE FOUNDATION OF EVERYTHING
THAT EXISTS, LOVE.

"

CONFUSION IS YOUR SOUL SHOWING YOU WHAT'S REAL, WHILE YOUR CONDITIONED MIND DOESN'T WANT TO BELIEVE IT.

YOUR THOUGHTS AND TALKS WITH SELF ARE CONVERSATIONS WITH GOD. BE MINDFUL OF THEM.

YOUR DECISIONS DON'T NEED TO MAKE SENSE TO ANYONE ELSE AS LONG AS IT IS WHAT'S RIGHT FOR YOUR GROWTH.

"

DECISIONS ARE THE DRIVING FORCE IN
GROWTH. THE HARDEST ONES ARE USUALLY
THE MOST REWARDING.

THE DEEP-DOWN FEELING THAT YOU KNOW IS
RIGHT EVEN IF IT SEEMS WRONG TO EVERYONE
ELSE. THE THING YOU KNOW YOU HAVE TO DO,
EVEN IF YOU DON'T WANT TO DO IT. THAT IS
YOUR INTUITION, LISTEN TO IT.

CHANGE YOUR DEFINITION OF WHAT MIRACLES
ARE, AND YOU'LL EXPERIENCE MORE OF THEM.

DETACHING AND CUTTING THE CORD DOESN'T MEAN THE LOVE WAS NEVER REAL, IT SIMPLY MEANS YOU CHOSE TO LOVE YOURSELF, WHILE ANOTHER MAKES THEIR OWN DESTRUCTIVE DECISIONS.

'I DIDN'T TRULY LOVE MYSELF, IN TURN, NOT LOVING THEM PROPERLY BY PLACING EXPECTATIONS ON THEM TO FULFILL MY OWN NEEDS' - #PEOPLELIKEUS

IF YOUR LIFE IS CONSTANTLY SURROUNDED BY DISLOYALTY AND DRAMA, YOU MUST LOOK INWARD TO SEE WHY. YOUR ENERGY, DECISIONS, ACTIONS AND THOUGHTS ATTRACT EVERYTHING IN YOUR LIFE.

"

IF WE ARE DOING THINGS THAT DISRESPECT OUR OWN BODY, MIND AND SOUL, WHY WOULD WE EXPECT ANOTHER TO RESPECT OUR BODY, MIND AND SOUL?

DO NOT ALLOW ANOTHER PERSON'S OPINION CREATE SELF-DOUBT AND LACK OF MOTIVATION. RELEASE THE PROJECT. DO THE THING THEY SAY YOU ARE NOT CAPABLE OF.

DO NOT CONTINUE TO BE ANGERED BY A PERSON FROM A PAST RELATIONSHIP, THEY WERE PLACED IN FRONT OF YOU AS A LESSON, YOUR CONTINUED ANGER IS YOUR REFUSAL TO LEARN SAID LESSON.

“

DO NOT APOLOGIZE, WHEN APOLOGIZING ISN’T
NECESSARY.

DO NOT HINDER YOUR GROWTH, IN FEAR OF
OUTGROWING THOSE AROUND YOU.

NEVER LET ANOTHER TELL YOU HOW TO FEEL.
THEY ARE YOUR FEELINGS. THEY ARE VALID,
AND YOU’RE THE OWNER OF THEM, NOBODY
ELSE.

DON’T LOSE FAITH IN HUMANITY UNLESS YOU,
YOURSELF, HAVE MADE A DECISION TO REMAIN
AS YOU ARE.

"

ONCE YOU GENUINELY LOVE YOURSELF, YOU DON'T WANT TO DO UNHEALTHY THINGS TO YOUR BODY, YOU DON'T WANT TO DISRESPECT YOUR BODY, YOU WILL MAKE DECISIONS THAT ALIGN WITH THAT MENTALITY. ONCE YOU LOVE YOURSELF, YOU HAVE NO OTHER FEELINGS TOWARD ANOTHER, BESIDES LOVE, BECAUSE THAT IS NOW WHAT RESIDES WITHIN YOU.

DRASTIC CHANGE IN A PERSON CAN PLACE FEAR IN THOSE THAT ARE CLOSE TO THEM. IT IS AN UNKNOWN TERRITORY AND WE HAVE BEEN TAUGHT TO FIND FEAR IN THE UNKNOWN.

STOP ALLOWING OTHERS TO DULL YOUR SPARKLE DUE TO THEIR LACK OF SHINE, AND THEIR LACK OF WANT TO CHANGE.

"

AN EGO-BASED DECISION IS THE ONE THAT MAKES SENSE. AN INTUITION-BASED DECISION IS THE LEAST APPEALING, BUT THE ONE YOU KNOW IS RIGHT.

ELEVATE YOUR MIND. INCREASE YOUR KNOWLEDGE. FIGHT FROM A FOUNDATION OF LOVE. IT'S THE ONLY WAY THE WORLD HAS A CHANCE. THE ONLY WAY TO DO THIS FOR THE WORLD, IS TO FIRST FIND LOVE FOR YOURSELF. FINDING LOVE FOR YOURSELF AGAIN, FINDS SELF-RESPECT, SELF-WORTH, AND SELF-ESTEEM. TO FIND THESE THINGS, YOU MUST UNDRESS EVERYTHING ABOUT YOURSELF CURRENTLY, AND CLOTHE YOURSELF WITH HONESTY. AFTER THIS CHANGE, AN OUTSIDE SOURCE CANNOT TRIGGER A NEGATIVE FEELING WITHIN YOU.

“

EMOTIONS ARE MEANT TO BE FELT. EMOTIONS
ARE MEANT TO BE RELEASED. THIS IS THE WAY
TO GENUINE PEACE, NOT JUST PRETENDING TO
BE HAPPY ALL THE TIME.

IT IS IMPOSSIBLE ENERGETICALLY, FOR A SOURCE
OUTSIDE OF YOURSELF TO FILL A VOID WITHIN
YOURSELF. ONLY YOU CAN DO THAT.

EVERY ACTION WE TAKE TOWARD PEOPLE,
REFLECTS OUR OWN FEELINGS TOWARD
OURSELVES.

"

EVERY PERSON IN YOUR LIFE IS MEANT TO BE LOOKED INTO LIKE A MIRROR. EVERY PERSON IS YOU, AND IS MEANT TO HELP YOU REMEMBER WHO YOU ARE.

EVERYBODY IS HURTING. THE WORLD IS A PLACE OF GOOD VERSUS EVIL. START BEING HONEST WITH YOURSELF, SO THAT YOU MAY LOVE YOURSELF, HEAL YOURSELF, AND BECOME YOUR BEST SELF, FOR THE GOOD OF THE WORLD.

EVERYONE LOVES INSPIRATION UNTIL IT INVOLVES SHINING LIGHT ON THEIR SHADOWS. REVEALING HIDDEN TRUTHS DOESN'T HAVE TO BE YOUR DEATH, BUT RATHER, YOUR REBIRTH.

"

EVERY ACTION YOU TAKE WHILE EXPRESSING
UNCONDITIONAL LOVE TOWARD ANOTHER,
MUST ALSO EXPRESS UNCONDITIONAL LOVE
FOR YOURSELF. IF IT'S ONLY GOOD FOR ONE OF
YOU, IT'S NOT TRUE UNCONDITIONAL LOVE.

THE FEAR OF REALIZING EVERYTHING ABOUT
YOU, ISN'T REALLY YOU, WILL HOLD YOU
CAPTIVE. RELEASE YOUR FEAR.

'I WANTED TO KEEP CONTROL OF THE
SITUATION, BECAUSE THAT'S WHERE I FELT SAFE,
IN CONTROL.' - #PEOPLELIKEUS

"

FIND THE BEAUTY IN YOUR SOUL, IT RESTS ON THE OTHER SIDE OF HONESTY. WE HAVE PLAYED A ROLE IN EVERY SITUATION PRESENTED IN OUR LIVES. SEE HOW YOU ALONE, COULD HAVE CHANGED A WHOLE SCENARIO, JUST BY CHANGING YOUR REACTION TO IT. RECOGNIZE THE ROLE YOU'VE PLAYED, TAKE RESPONSIBILITY FOR IT, AND LEARN THE LESSONS INVOLVED TO AVOID REPEATING THE CYCLE.

THE FIRST STEP, IS REMEMBERING YOU'RE SPECIAL.

YOU ARE FLYING HIGH RIGHT NOW. THIS MAY THREATEN OTHERS. DO NOT DESCEND.

'I FORGAVE MYSELF FOR THE NEGATIVITY I BROUGHT TO THEM, JUST AS I FORGAVE THEM FOR THEIR ACTIONS TOWARD ME.' -
#PEOPLELIKEUS

"

FORGIVE YOURSELF.

"

YOUR GENUINE DREAMS AND DESIRES, ARE
MEMORIES OF WHO YOU REALLY ARE AND
WHAT YOU ARE TRULY HERE TO DO.

WHAT HAS BEEN TAUGHT TO US AS 'GOALS'
NECESSARY FOR SUCCESS, ISN'T SUCCESS AT ALL,
FOR IT IS PART OF AN ILLUSION, WHICH CAN BE
TAKEN AWAY. TRUE SUCCESS IS YOU, AND CAN
NEVER BE TAKEN AWAY.

THE UNIVERSE CANNOT BLESS YOU WITH
GRAND OPPORTUNITIES AND TRUE
ADVANCEMENT ON YOUR PATH, IF YOU'RE
ENGAGING IN ACTIVITIES THAT DIMINISH YOUR
SELF-WORTH, AND DIMINISH YOUR NATURAL
ABILITIES.

"

'I HAD TO BE HONEST WITH MYSELF AND ADMIT
THAT MY OWN KNOWLEDGE AND CHOICES IS
WHAT GOT ME WHERE I DIDN'T WANT TO BE, SO
MY SOURCE OF KNOWLEDGE HAD TO CHANGE.'
- #PEOPLELIKEUS

WHEN YOU FIND HAPPINESS WITHIN YOURSELF,
IT CANNOT BE TAKEN AWAY FROM YOU,
BECAUSE IT IS YOU.

YOU CANNOT WAIT FOR HAPPINESS TO HEAL
YOU. YOU MUST HEAL YOURSELF TO FIND
HAPPINESS.

"

HEALING ISN'T A ONE STEP PROCESS, IT'S A CONTINUOUS PROCESS, UNTIL THE FOUNDATION OF WHO YOU WERE TAUGHT TO BE IS BROKEN, AND THE FOUNDATION OF WHO YOU REALLY ARE EMERGES. BE PATIENT WITH YOURSELF.

THE FIRST STEP YOU CAN TAKE TO HELP THE WORLD, IS TO KEEP YOUR THOUGHTS POSITIVE. RELEASE HATE

RELEASE ANGER

RELEASE FEAR

THE ONLY TRUE EXISTENT ENERGY IS LOVE, FEAR WAS TAUGHT. GET BACK TO LOVE, TO REMEMBER WHO YOU ARE.

"

THOSE WHO HOLD GRUDGES TOWARD FAMILY
MEMBERS, ARE FILLED WITH ANGER TOWARD
THEMSELVES. BEFORE JUDGING ANOTHER AND
SPEAKING NEGATIVELY, BEFORE CONJURING UP
YOUR OWN TRUTH, LOOK AT YOUR OWN LACK
OF PERFECTION.

HONESTY WITH YOURSELF, ABOUT YOURSELF, IS
THE ONLY WAY TO ENSURE YOU WILL CREATE A
DIFFERENT OUTCOME BY CHANGING THE ROOT
OF YOUR THOUGHTS. YOU CANNOT CHANGE
WHAT YOU DO NOT ADMIT TO.

IF WE DON'T HUMBLE OURSELVES, WE WILL BE
PRESENTED WITH SITUATIONS THAT FORCE US
TO BE SUBMISSIVE.

"

THE BIBLE WAS TAUGHT USING THE SAME STRATEGY THAT WAS USED TO TAKE OVER LANDS AND FORCE RELIGION UPON THE NATIVES OF THOSE LANDS. THEY HAD TO CHOOSE RELIGION OR DEATH. THE BIBLE GIVES YOU A CHOICE, 'OBEY THIS BOOK OR BURN IN HELL.' THIS IS NOT A TEACHING OF GOD AND YOU MUST ACKNOWLEDGE THAT FIRST, TO CHANGE YOUR PERCEPTION OF THIS LIFE.

'I BROKE DOWN IN HUMBLE APPRECIATION FOR THE PROTECTION THAT GOD/UNIVERSE HAS HAD OVER ME, PRESERVING MY LIFE FOR THIS VERY OPPORTUNITY, WHEN I REMEMBERED ALL THE TIMES I COULD HAVE BEEN GONE.'

- #PEOPLELIKEUS

"

'I CATCH MYSELF APOLOGIZING FOR THINGS I HAVEN'T EVEN DONE WRONG. BY DOING THIS I ALLOW OTHERS TO ESCAPE THE REALITY OF THINGS THEY'VE DONE WRONG.'

WE NEED TO STOP TAKING BLAME FOR THINGS OTHERS HAVE DONE WRONG, TO PLEASE THEIR EGO.

-   #PEOPLELIKEUS

I LOVE YOU

DOESN'T HAVE TO BE A WEIRD FEELING, BUT A NATURAL FEELING, THAT WE SHOULD FEEL TOWARD ONE ANOTHER IN EVERYDAY LIFE

“

I USED TO ARGUE BECAUSE I THOUGHT I WAS ALWAYS RIGHT. BY ARGUING, I WAS REALLY SAYING, 'I WANT TO BELIEVE I'M RIGHT, SO LET ME PLACE MY OPINION IN YOU FORCEFULLY.

ALWAYS TRUST YOURSELF, IF YOU FEEL LIKE YOU CAN'T TRUST SOMEONE, YOU CAN'T.

IF YOU TRULY LOVE SOMEONE, YOU SHOULD WANT THEM TO GROW WITH OR WITHOUT YOUR PRESENCE.

'I'M NOT PREJUDICE BUT….' – THE 'BUT' MEANS YOU'RE PREJUDICE

"

WHEN YOU IGNORE YOUR INTUITION FOR SO LONG, AND AVOID MAKING NECESSARY DECISIONS, THE UNIVERSE WILL SAY, ENOUGH IS ENOUGH, AND FORCE A DECISION UPON YOU.

'...YOU ARE ABLE TO HEAL ANOTHER'S WOUNDS WHILE YOU, YOURSELF, ARE BLEEDING.

\-   #PEOPLELIKEUS

YOU AREN'T THE BAD THINGS YOU'VE DONE. YOU DID THEM BECAUSE YOU FORGOT WHO YOU ARE. NOW IS THE TIME TO REMEMBER.

"

WE CANNOT CONTINUE TO LIVE BY 'WHAT IFS'
THESE ARE NON-EXISTENT CIRCUMSTANCES
THAT WILL PREVENT CHANGE AND HINDER
GROWTH.

'MY GOAL ISN'T TO BE THE MOST INSPIRATIONAL
AUTHOR, BUT THE MOST HONEST.
ENCOURAGING OTHERS TO DO THE SAME.
BECAUSE CHANGE BEGINS WITH TRUTH.'

- GOODREADS.COM INTERVIEW

TO FIND ANGER INSTEAD OF GROWTH IN THE
SITUATIONS YOU'VE EXPERIENCED THIS YEAR,
WILL ENSURE THAT YOU REPEAT SIMILAR
EXPERIENCES NEXT YEAR.

"

WHEN YOU OVERCOME YOUR HARDSHIPS, YOU
CAN THEN SHOW OTHERS HOW TO, AND THAT
MY DEAR, IS HOW WE CHANGE THE WORLD.

WHEN YOU UNLEARN EVERYTHING, YOU THINK
YOU KNOW ABOUT LIFE, LIFE BECOMES EASIER
TO UNDERSTAND.

WE CAN BECOME SO DEFINED BY OUR PAST
THAT WE ARE FEARFUL OF WHO WE ARE
WITHOUT OUR STRUGGLES. TAKE AWAY THE
PAST, AND SOME WOULD FEEL LIKE THEY DO
NOT EXIST.

"

THERE IS NO SUCH THING AS FAILURE, ONLY LESSONS TO BE LEARNED, AND DIFFERENT PATHS MEANT TO BE TAKEN.

IT'S THE SMALLEST ACTS OF LOVE, LIKE LISTENING TO SOMEONE AND REALLY PAYING ATTENTION TO WHAT THEY HAVE TO SAY, THAT HELPS PEOPLE FLOURISH. CHILD OR ADULT, WE ALL JUST WANT TO BE LOVED AND ACCEPTED FOR WHO WE ARE.

GOD DOESN'T PUNISH PEOPLE BY SENDING THEM TO A FIERY PIT CALLED HELL, THAT IS A FEAR TACTIC PLACED UPON US SO THAT WE ABIDE BY RULES FROM A BOOK, THAT WAS CREATED TO LEAD US TO THE ACCEPTANCE OF OUR OWN DESTRUCTION.

"

WE MUST TAKE RESPONSIBILITY FOR THE ROLE
WE HAVE PLAYED IN PEOPLES LIVES, IN A
NEGATIVE MANNER, AND REALIZE, THAT THE
NEGATIVE SITUATIONS WE ENCOUNTER, ARE A
RESULT OF THOSE NEGATIVE ROLES WE'VE
PLAYED IN THE LIVES OF OTHERS.

#PEOPLELIKEUS ARE CAPABLE OF LOVING THOSE
THAT OTHERS DEEM UNWORTHY, BECAUSE WE
KNOW, EVERYBODY IS DESERVING OF LOVE, BUT
WE FORGET THAT WE ARE ALSO DESERVING OF
LOVE.

IN OUR PURSUIT OF OBTAINING THE THINGS
TAUGHT TO US AS IMPORTANT, WE LOSE
OURSELVES, OUR SOULS AND OUR PHYSICAL
LIFE.

"

WE ARE ALL HERE TO HELP EACH OTHER
REMEMBER WHO WE ARE. CHANGE IS THE KEY
NEEDED TO UNLOCK THE MEMORY.

YOU ARE NOT STUCK. YOU ARE HERE FOR
MORE.

A PERSON CAN ONLY RESPECT YOU AT THE
SAME LEVEL YOU RESPECT YOURSELF.

"

IT IS ENERGETICALLY IMPOSSIBLE TO BECOME
WHO YOU ARE MEANT TO BE, WHILE REMAINING
WHO YOU CURRENTLY ARE.

GROWTH IS FOUND AT THE BOTTOM OF THE
BASEMENT, WHERE NOBODY WANTS TO GO
BECAUSE IT'S DARK, STAGNANT, AND
UNCOMFORTABLE.

UNLOCK THE MEMORY OF WHO YOU ARE, BY
LETTING GO OF WHO YOU ARE NOT.

"

WE MUST STOP KEEPING PEOPLE CONTAINED BY
THEIR PAST ACTIONS, AND ALLOW EACH OTHER
TO GROW.

"

THE NEED TO PROVE TO ANOTHER THAT YOU ARE ENOUGH, IS PROOF THAT YOU DON'T BELIEVE IT YOURSELF.

THE LACK OF LOVE AND APPRECIATION YOU FEEL FROM OTHERS, IS DIRECTLY REFLECTING THE LACK OF LOVE AND APPRECIATION YOU HAVE FOR YOURSELF.

IF YOUR GOALS IN LIFE AREN'T WORKING OUT, ITS BECAUSE YOU ARE HERE TO DO SOMETHING COMPLETELY DIFFERENT THAN WHAT YOU ARE CURRENTLY STRIVING FOR. YOU ARE MORE THAN JUST BEAUTIFUL; YOU HAVE SOMETHING ELSE TO OFFER THE WORLD. LISTEN TO YOURSELF.

LOVE, ACE

(A PERSONAL MESSAGE DELIVERED TO A FRIEND FROM ACE BABY AFTER HE PASSED)

"

YOU CANNOT EXPECT A DIFFERENT LIFE WITH BETTER END RESULTS, WHILE USING THE SAME DESTRUCTIVE MENTALITY TO MAKE YOUR DECISIONS.

WISDOM TO KNOW THE DIFFERENCE BETWEEN WHAT WE CAN AND CANNOT CHANGE IS A SIMPLE CONCEPT. IF IT IS A SITUATION, YOU CAN CHANGE IT, BY HOW YOU PERCEIVE IT OR REMOVING YOURSELF FROM IT. IF IT IS A PERSON, YOU CANNOT CHANGE IT. KNOWING THAT IS THE WISDOM THAT SOME WILL NEVER COME TO POSSESS.

'I LEARNED THAT I'M ATTRACTING THESE TYPES OF MEN INTO MY LIFE BECAUSE WHAT RESIDES IN THEM, ALSO RESIDES IN ME.'

\-   #PEOPLELIKEUS

"

THE UNIVERSE WILL ALLOW THINGS TO HAPPEN TO PLACE YOU BACK ON YOUR PATH, IF YOU'RE NOT MAKING THE RIGHT DECISIONS TO GET YOURSELF THERE.

WHEN NOTHING IS GOING RIGHT, IT'S TIME TO LOOK LEFT.

I HAD TO HAVE FAITH, BECAUSE I DIDN'T HAVE A PLAN.

THE ONLY WAY TO RELEASE THE NEED FOR CONTROL, IS TO HAVE FAITH, THE TWO CANNOT CO-EXIST.

"

YOU CANNOT FIND TRUE HAPPINESS IN THE COMPANY OF OTHERS, UNTIL YOU HAVE FOUND HAPPINESS IN YOUR OWN COMPANY.

AN ATTACHMENT TO A PERSON IS AN ADDICTION, AND IS NO DIFFERENT THAN AN ADDICTION TO A SUBSTANCE. IT IS UNHEALTHY, AND WILL CONTROL YOUR LIFE IF YOU ALLOW IT TO.

TRUE LOVE ALLOWS ONE TO FIND THEIR OWN PATH.

"

TURNING INWARD IS THE BEGINNING. THE
BEGINNING OF LIVING LIFE AS WE WERE
CREATED TO LIVE. LIFE IS A NEVER-ENDING
EVOLUTION OF SELF, THAT HAS NO PARTICULAR
DESTINATION TO REACH. THE DESTINATION LIES
IN THE JOURNEY THAT TAKES YOU TO NEW
LEVELS, WITH NEW LESSONS.

THE ANSWERS COME IN YOUR SILENCE. BE STILL.

DON'T KEEP PUSHING YOUR LIFE TO THE SIDE. IF
YOU DON'T MAKE TIME, THE UNIVERSE WILL
PRESENT YOU WITH TIME, IN A WAY THAT YOU
HAVE NO CONTROL OVER.

"

HAVING A PURE HEART CAN BE BEAUTIFUL, AND DISCOURAGING. PROTECT IT BY USING IT TO LOVE YOURSELF FIRST.

HOW TO FREE YOURSELF: REALIZE THAT YOU CAN

HOW YOU THINK YOUR LIFE SHOULD BE IS DIRECTLY AFFECTING HOW YOU FEEL ABOUT YOUR LIFE CURRENTLY, TAKING YOU AWAY FROM, EXPERIENCING LIFE.

"

HOW YOU REACT TO A PROBLEM, CAUSES JUST
AS MANY ISSUES AS THE ACTUAL PROBLEM.

I DON'T REGRET ANY LOVE THAT I HAVE GIVEN,
BECAUSE IT WAS NECESSARY AT THE TIME.

MOST ARE AGENDA DRIVEN AND WILL CHOOSE
YOU TO FILL A VOID WITHIN THEMSELVES. BE
SAFE.

'I KNOW BUT' IS ALREADY BLOCKING YOU FROM
HEARING THE MESSAGE.

"

WHEN YOU PLACE YOURSELF LAST, YOU ARE SHOWING OTHERS WHERE TO PLACE YOU IN THEIR LIVES…. LAST.

PEOPLE WILL HOLD THEMSELVES SUPERIOR TO OTHERS, IN ORDER TO HIDE THE INFERIOR LEVEL, THEY TRULY HOLD THEMSELVES AT.

THE FUTURE IS NONEXISTENT. IT IS CREATED BY THE DECISIONS YOU MAKE TODAY.

THE NEGATIVE ISSUES YOU FACE AREN'T REALISTICALLY NEGATIVE. THEY ARE OCCURRENCES THAT ARE BEING PERCEIVED AS NEGATIVE, BY YOU.

"

THE ONLY TRUE LIMITS YOU HAVE, ARE THE ONES YOU PLACE UPON YOURSELF, DUE TO THE LIMITING BELIEFS YOU WERE TAUGHT.

THERE IS A RESPECTFUL WAY TO EXIT A TOXIC RELATIONSHIP. DO THAT.

THE ACT OF NOT ACCEPTING ANOTHER FOR WHO THEY ARE, IS A DEMONSTRATION OF THE LACK OF ACCEPTANCE YOU HAVE FOR YOURSELF. WE ARE ALL ONE, FROM ONE SOURCE OF CREATION. TO DENY ANOTHER LOVE, IS TO ALSO DENY YOURSELF OF LOVE.

"

FOR THE PERSON THAT FEELS HELD PRISONER
RIGHT NOW:

IT HAS ALL BEEN PART OF YOUR JOURNEY. IT IS
NOW TIME TO RELEASE YOURSELF FROM THAT
PRISON, BY WALKING THROUGH THE DOORS
THAT HAVE ALWAYS BEEN OPEN.

"

WHAT YOU CHOOSE TO DO WITH YOUR
OBSTACLES WILL DETERMINE YOUR LIFE. LET
THEM BREAK YOU, YOU WILL REMAIN BROKEN.
LET THEM GROW YOU, YOU WILL EVOLVE.

WHEN THE JOB IS GONE, WHEN THE MONEY IS
GONE, WHEN THE PARTNER IS GONE, YOU ARE
ALL THAT REMAINS. LOVE YOU. LIVE FOR YOU.

IN THE SEARCH FOR ANOTHER TO LOVE YOU,
YOU WILL FIND THAT IT IS YOU, YOU'VE BEEN
SEARCHING FOR THE WHOLE TIME.

"

"IN MY INTRODUCTION, I WAS TOLD THAT I SOUNDED LIKE 'SOME SUPER ANGEL WHO CAME TO SAVE THE WORLD,' AND THAT I SHOULDN'T AIM FOR THAT. I THEN WATERED IT DOWN, AND IT NEVER SAT RIGHT WITH ME. I FELT LIKE THE WATERED-DOWN VERSION WAS COMPLETELY DEFEATING MY PURPOSE OF BEING MYSELF AND WAS DAMPENING MY PURSUIT OF ENCOURAGING OTHERS TO BE THEMSELVES, WITH NO REMORSE."

-   #PEOPLELIKEUS

IT IS NOT FOR YOU TO 'DECIDE' WHAT YOUR PURPOSE IS. IT IS FOR YOU TO REMEMBER, BY UNLEARNING EVERYTHING YOU WERE TAUGHT TO BE.

IT IS NOT YOUR JOB TO PROVIDE ANOTHER WITH HAPPINESS. THEY MUST ACHIEVE THAT ON THEIR OWN.

"

IT IS TIME.

DECISIONS MUST BE MADE TO AVOID
REPEATING THE SAME CYCLE YOU ARE TRYING
TO GET OUT OF.

JEALOUSY IS ONE'S FEAR THAT ANOTHER IS
BETTER THAN THEM.

BY LOVING OURSELVES, WE LEARN HOW
OTHERS SHOULD BE LOVING US. BY LOVING
OURSELVES, CLARITY COMES ON HOW MUCH
WE HAVEN'T GENUINELY LOVED OR BEEN
LOVED.

"

THE JOURNEY TO LOVING YOURSELF IS ONE
FILLED WITH SECRETS YOU NEVER WANTED TO
ADMIT TO. IT GETS UGLY AND HURTFUL, BUT
THE END RESULT IS MORE BEAUTIFUL THAN YOU
COULD EVER IMAGINE.

LEARN TO LOVE YOURSELF UNCONDITIONALLY,
SO THAT YOUR VALIDITY DOESN'T RELY ON
ANOTHER'S WANT FOR YOU.

LET GO OF WHAT YOU THOUGHT LIFE SHOULD
BE, AND ALLOW THE UNIVERSE TO LEAD YOU TO
WHERE YOUR LIFE IS SUPPOSED TO BE.

"

MY HEART'S DESIRE, MY SOUL MISSION ON
EARTH IS TO HELP YOU SEE THAT YOU ARE HERE
FOR A REASON, YOU ARE SPECIAL, YOU ARE
IMPORTANT AND YOU ARE NEEDED. I HAVE
LIVED THROUGH MY EXPERIENCES SO THAT I
CAN ASSURE YOU THAT YOU ARE NOT ALONE IN
YOUR STRUGGLES. THERE IS HOPE, AND IT ALL
BEGINS WITHIN YOURSELF.

LOVE, SHANNA

"

LEAVING YOUR PROBLEMS IN THE HANDS OF
THE LORD, ALLOWS YOU TO PLACE
RESPONSIBILITY FOR YOUR LIFE, ON AN OUTSIDE
SOURCE. YOU WILL NEVER FIX YOUR INTERNAL
ISSUES, AS LONG AS YOU DEPEND ON AN
OUTSIDE SOURCE TO DO IT FOR YOU. YOU ARE
YOUR OWN SALVATION, WHEN YOU DECIDE TO
ACCEPT RESPONSIBILITY.

ALLOWING YOUR PAST TRAUMA TO DEFINE
YOU, IS TRAUMATIZING TO YOUR PRESENT
REALITY.

LIFE CAN BE STRESSFUL OR EFFORTLESS. YOU
CHOOSE WHICH ONE BY HOW YOU PERCEIVE
EVERYDAY OCCURRENCES, BY THE DECISIONS
YOU MAKE, AND THE BOUNDARIES YOU SET.

"

'… YOUR LIFE IS A MIRROR UNTO YOU AND
ONLY YOU. WHAT YOUR MIND PROJECTS, YOUR
LIFE PLAYS OUT IN ACTION.'
-    #PEOPLELIKEUS

YOU HAVE LIT ENOUGH CANDLES FOR OTHERS,
ITS TIME TO LIGHT YOUR OWN, SO YOU CAN
CHINE AS YOU WERE INTENDED TO.

WHEN YOU CAN'T STOP LIVING IN THE PAST,
YOU'VE ALREADY FAILED YOUR FUTURE.

LOGIC WILL KEEP YOU FROM EXPERIENCING THE
MAGIC THAT YOU ARE.

"

WE SHOULD BE LIVING LIFE AS IT HAPPENS, AND
LET THE UNIVERSE /GOD, GUIDE OUR EVERY
DECISION, INSTEAD OF CREATING
UNNECESSARY STRESS BY TRYING TO FORCE
OUR OWN EXPECTATIONS OF A SPECIFIC LIFE.

WHEN YOU TRULY REMEMBER WHO YOU ARE,
AND LOVE EVERY PART OF YOURSELF, YOU ARE
NO LONGER CAPABLE OF DOING THINGS THAT
YOU WILL BE ASHAMED OF BECAUSE YOU
FOUND SELF-WORTH. BE A WORK IN PROGRESS,
NOT A MEDIOCRE FINISHED PRODUCT.

LOVE IS NOT POSSESSION.

"

LOVE IS NOT SACRIFICE OF ONE'S HAPPINESS, IN THE HOPES OF BRINGING ANOTHER HAPPINESS.

TO LOVE WITH NO ATTACHMENT IS THE PUREST UNCONDITIONAL LOVE YOU CAN GIVE. TO UNDERSTAND AND ACCEPT THAT A PERSON DOESN'T BELONG TO YOU, BUT YOU LOVE THEM ANYWAYS, IS GENUINE LOVE.

BY DRAWING A LINE, CREATING A BOUNDARY WITH PEOPLE THAT MISUSE YOUR LOVE, YOU ARE LOVING YOURSELF MORE THAN THAT PERSON FOR ONCE.

"

MASTERING YOURSELF IS THE CHANGE THE
WORLD NEEDS.

WHEN A MEMORY TRIGGERS A NEGATIVE
EMOTION, BE IT SADNESS OR ANGER, THIS IS
SHOWING YOU THAT YOU HAVE YET TO
COMPLETELY RELEASE THE NEGATIVITY
ATTACHED TO THAT MEMORY. THIS EMOTION
WILL CONTINUE TO ARISE UNTIL YOU
COMPLETELY RELEASE IT.

A MOTHER IS A SONS FIRST PERCEPTION OF
LOVE AND HIS FIRST EXAMPLE OF HOW A
WOMAN SHOULD BEHAVE.

"

'... MY SOUL STILL CRAVED THE CONNECTION TO AN ENERGY ON THE SAME LEVEL AS MINE, REMINDING ME, THAT I SHOULD NOT CRAVE ANOTHER BEING BECAUSE I MYSELF, AM ENOUGH.'

-    #PEOPLELIKEUS

THE NEED FOR ANOTHER'S ATTENTION REFLECTS THE LACK OF ATTENTION YOU GIVE YOURSELF.

LOVE AND TEND TO YOUR NEEDS.

YOUR NEGATIVE PERCEPTION OF ANOTHER IS REVEALING THE NEGATIVE PERCEPTION YOU HOLD OF YOURSELF. YOUR NEGATIVE PERCEPTION OF ANOTHER, CAN BE A FEAR OF LACKING SOMETHING THAT ANOTHER POSSESSES.

"

YOU CAN NO LONGER HIDE FROM YOUR HEART AND SOUL, YOU MUST SPEAK YOUR TRUTHS, OR LIGHT WILL BE CAST UPON YOUR SHADOWS. IT'S TIME FOR HONESTY.

NO MATTER WHO SAYS IT'S RIGHT, IF IT FEELS WRONG, IT IS. LISTEN TO YOUR INTUITION.

IF THERE WERE NO RELIGION, THERE WOULD BE LESS JUDGEMENT AMONGST HUMANITY.

"

THERE'S NO ROOM FOR ANYTHING NEW, IF YOU CAN'T LET GO OF ANYTHING OLD. THERE'S NO ROOM FOR GROWTH WITHOUT CHANGE.

THERE IS NO SUCH THING AS 'COINCIDENCE.' EVERY SITUATION IN LIFE IS PROVIDED FOR YOU TO USE AS A STEP CLOSER TO REMEMBERING WHO YOU ARE. HOWEVER, REACTING THE SAME WAY TO EVERY SITUATION, EVERY TIME IT OCCURS, YOU WILL NEVER LEARN THE LESSON, AND NEVER MOVE FORWARD WITHIN YOURSELF.

NOBODY CAN OUTSHINE YOU ONCE YOU SEE THE LIGHT YOU ARE TO THE WORLD.

"

NOBODY WANTS TO DECLUTTER INTERNALLY, BECAUSE IN ORDER TO DECLUTTER, IT MUST FIRST BE ACKNOWLEDGED THAT THERE'S A MESS.

IT IS NOT ANYBODY ELSE'S JOB TO SAVE YOU. EVEN IF YOU SACRIFICED YOUR ENTIRE BEING FOR OTHERS, THAT WAS YOUR CHOICE, NOT THEIR OBLIGATION TO REPAY YOU. ITS TIME TO SAVE YOURSELF.

BY NOT GENUINELY FORGIVING A PERSON, YOU ARE HOLDING THEM CAPTIVE TI THE ACTION THAT YOU CAN'T FORGIVE THEM FOR. THIS CAPTIVITY WILL PREVENT THEM FROM GROWING.

"

YOU ARE NOT HERE TO PLEASE ANOTHER. YOUR
PURPOSE IS FAR GREATER.

YOU CAN SHOW A PERSON THE WAY. IT IS NOT
YOUR BUSINESS WHAT THEY DO WITH THE
INFORMATION.

NOTHING HAS POWER OVER YOU WITHOUT
YOUR CONSENT

"

DEFINITION OF AN OBSTACLE:

PREVENTS OR HINDERS PROGRESS

THE UNIVERSE DOESN'T PRESENT OBSTACLES. THE UNIVERSE PRESENTS OPPORTUNITIES TO VIEW YOUR SITUATION DIFFERENT, WHICH WOULD LEAD TO PROGRESS.

YOU CHOOSE HOW TO VIEW YOUR SITUATION, OBSTACLE VS. OPPORTUNITY

THE ONLY WAY TO RIDE A WAVE IS TO GO WITH IT. GOING AGAINST A WAVE WILL ONLY EXHAUST YOU WHILE REMAINING IN THE SAME PLACE.

"

ANOTHER PERSON CAN ONLY HELP YOU BASED ON WHAT YOU TELL THEM. ONLY YOU CAN HELP YOURSELF BASED ON ACKNOWLEDGING YOUR TRUTHS.

ONLY YOU HAVE THE POWER TO TRANSFORM YOUR MIND. THAT MAKES YOU THE CREATOR OR DESTROYER OF YOUR DESTINY.

OTHER PEOPLE DO NOT ANGER YOU. YOUR UNHEALED WOUNDS ARE BEING OPENED. TEND TO THOSE.

“

OPEN THE BOX YOUR MIND HAS BEEN PLACED
IN, AND SEE THE FREEDOM THAT YOUR MIND
TRULY POSSESSES. ONCE YOU UNLEARN THE LIES,
YOU WILL NO LONGER BE EASILY MANIPULATED.
THIS IS HOW THE WORLD ASCENDS.

WHEN YOU LOVE YOURSELF, OTHERS WILL SEE
HOW TO LOVE YOU. THE ONES THAT MATTER
WILL LEARN; THE ONES THAT DON'T WILL LEAVE.

OUR LOVE, WHEN NOT DIRECTED CORRECTLY,
CAN HOLD SOMEONE CAPTIVE, NOT ALLOWING
THEM TO GROW. WE ARE DEMANDING
GROWTH, WHILE NOT GIVING THE SPACE FOR IT.

"

A SOURCE OUTSIDE OF YOU, CANNOT CREATE
SOMETHING WITHIN YOU, IT ALREADY EXISTS.

ALL OF THE EMOTIONS YOU FEEL TOWARD
YOUR PAST ARE VALID, HOWEVER, YOU DO NOT
HAVE TO ALLOW THEM TO DEFINE OR JUSTIFY
YOUR CURRENT ACTIONS.

YOU CAN BE SHOWN THE SAME PICTURE AS
ANOTHER PERSON, AND SEE A DIFFERENT
IMAGE, THIS IS PERCEPTION. YOU AND I CAN
EXPERIENCE THE SAME OCCURRENCES IN OUR
LIVES, BUT HOW WE PERCEIVE IT CAN CREATE
TOTALLY DIFFERENT REALITIES

"

PEOPLE LIKE US WERE PLACED HERE TO SEE THE
BEAUTY IN BROKEN PEOPLE AND SHARE LOVE
WITH THEM SO THEY MAY HEAL. BUT WE CAN
ONLY HELP OTHERS HEAL, BY FIRST HEALING
OURSELVES. WE CAN ONLY LOVE OTHERS
GENUINELY, BY FIRST LOVING OURSELVES
GENUINELY.

"

ALL I CAN DO IS POINT YOU IN THE RIGHT
DIRECTION. YOU MUST TAKE ACTION TO WALK
THE PATH, IT IS YOUR OWN.

IN LOVING YOURSELF, EVERY ASPECT OF
YOURSELF, YOU'LL WANT TO KEEP YOUR
THOUGHTS POSITIVE. THEY ARE ABOUT YOU,
FROM YOU, TO YOU.

REALISTICALLY, THERE ARE NO OTHERS. EVERY
OCCURRENCE IN YOUR LIFE, IS A
MANIFESTATION OF YOU.

"

THERE IS A PATH FOR YOUR LIFE, THAT HAS BEEN LAID OUT FOR YOU SINCE THE MOMENT OF YOUR BIRTH. IT IS ON THIS PATH, THAT YOU WILL EXPERIENCE GENUINE HAPPINESS, AS IT IS YOUR SOULS' PURPOSE OF EXISTENCE IN THIS LIFE TIME. IT IS FEAR OF THE UNKNOWN, THAT WILL KEEP YOU FROM THIS PATH, BECAUSE LOGICAL DECISIONS WILL BE MADE, THAT LEAD YOU TO WHAT WE'VE BEEN TAUGHT WE'RE SUPPOSED TO ACCOMPLISH, INSTEAD OF INTUITIVE ONES, THAT ARE DIVINELY GUIDING YOU FROM OUR SOURCE OF CREATION.

"

NO MATTER HOW PURE YOUR INTENTIONS ARE, PEOPLE CAN ONLY PERCEIVE YOU FROM THEIR OWN LEVEL OF THINKING. CONTINUE TO MOVE FORWARD, YOU CANNOT FORCE THE TRUTH UPON ONE WHO DOES NOT WANT TO RECEIVE IT.

'... IF WE DON'T PUT BOUNDARIES INTO PLACE, WE'LL ALLOW OUR OWN LIGHT TO DIM, IN EFFORTS OF UNCOVERING SOMEONE ELSE'S.

WHEN YOU REALIZE HOW BEAUTIFUL YOU ARE ON THE INSIDE, PERCEPTION OF YOUR OUTSIDE WILL CHANGE.

"

ANGER AND HATRED ARE A RECIPE FOR YOUR DEMISE. HEALTH ISSUES ARE EMOTIONAL ISSUES, MANIFESTED IN THE PHYSICAL REALM.

RELEASE ANY REGRET YOU HAVE OF ANY DECISIONS OR ACTIONS IN YOUR LIFE THUS FAR, FOR THEY HAVE BROUGHT YOU TO THIS POINT.

RELEASING YOUR NEGATIVE PAST MAKES ROOM FOR A POSITIVE FUTURE.

"

IN RELEASING ALL THAT NO LONGER SERVES YOU, YOU WILL FIND THAT ALL THERE IS LEFT TO DO, IS LIVE.

WHEN WE PLACE OURSELVES IN THE ROLE OF THE VICTIM, WE AUTOMATICALLY TAKE AWAY OUR OWN POWER TO FREE OURSELVES.

TO SACRIFICE LISTENING TO YOUR OWN SOUL CALLING YOU TO BE WHO YOU ARE, IN HOPES OF PLEASING ANOTHER, WILL TAKE YOU FURTHER AWAY FROM HAPPINESS

"

IF YOU MUST SACRIFICE HONESTY FOR
ACCEPTANCE, YOU ARE IN THE WRONG
ENVIRONMENT.

THE SAME THING YOU DON'T LIKE IN ANOTHER,
RESIDES WITHIN YOURSELF. RELEASE PRIDE &
ACKNOWLEDGE THE REASON PEOPLE ARE
PLACED IN FRONT OF YOU.

WE ARE HERE TO SHOW OTHERS THE BEAUTY
THEY DON'T SEE IN THEMSELVES.

"

PEOPLE ARE SCARED TO BELIEVE THAT WHAT THEY'VE BEEN TAUGHT THEIR WHOLE LIFE IS FALSE. LET FEAR GO SO YOU CAN OPEN YOUR MIND AND SEE PASSED THE LIES.

YOU CAN SHOW PEOPLE THEIR WORTH, WITHOUT SACRIFICING YOUR OWN.

EVERY SITUATION ONLY HAS AS MUCH POWER AS YOU GIVE IT. A PERSON CAN ONLY HAVE POWER OVER YOU, IF YOU ALLOW THEM TO.

"

THE UNIVERSE WILL ALWAYS REWARD YOUR
COMPLAINING SPIRIT WITH SOMETHING TO
COMPLAIN ABOUT.

IT IS TIME TO STOP PLAYING THE VICTIM, AND
ACKNOWLEDGE THE ROLE YOU HAVE PLAYED
IN THE WAY PEOPLE TREAT YOU.

HAVE YOU EVER SEEN A SURFER CATCH A
SUCCESSFUL WAVE?

ME NEITHER.

"

YOUR SOUL KNOWS WHAT'S GOOD FOR YOUR SOUL. EVERYTHING ELSE YOU ARE CONTEMPLATING, IS JUST THAT, CONTEMPLATION CREATED IN YOUR MIND, BY YOU. FOLLOW YOUR SOUL.

WHEN YOU HAVE DONE EVERYTHING THAT YOU THOUGHT WOULD MAKE YOU HAPPY, AND STILL FEEL EMPTY INSIDE, LET THE UNIVERSE TAKE OVER. THAT IS YOU AT THE HIGHEST VERSION OF EXISTENCE, THAT IS ONE WITH THE SOURCE OF CREATION, THAT IS GOD.

"

STRESS AND ANXIETY ARE YOUR MIND TRYING
TO USE LOGIC TO MEET THE EXPECTATIONS OF
WHAT YOU THINK YOUR LIFE SHOULD BE. WHO
YOU ARE HERE TO BE VERSUS WHO YOU WERE
TOLD TO BE, WILL KEEP YOU IN AN INFINITE
STATE OF STRESS AND ANXIETY.

"

HEALING SHOULD NOT BECOME AN INFINITE
STATE OF BEING IN ONE LIFE TIME. GENUINE
HEALING WOULD REBUILD ONE'S FOUNDATION
OF EXISTENCE. TO REBUILD THE FOUNDATION
OF ONE'S EXISTENCE, THAT IS THE
SUBCONSCIOUS, WOULD BE TO REBUILD THE
PLACE IN WHICH EVERY THOUGHT AND ACTION
IS FORMED. AT THIS LEVEL, WHERE HEALING IS
COMPLETE, TEARS ARE NO LONGER OF SADNESS,
BUT RATHER, GRATITUDE.

"

YOU HAVE THE ABILITY TO INSPIRE PEOPLE EVERY DAY, IN A WAY THAT NOBODY ELSE IN THE WORLD CAN, JUST BY BEING YOURSELF.

THE DEFENSIVE PERSON IS THE GUILTY PERSON.

IF A PERSON IS EASILY OFFENDED, ITS DUE TO THEIR GUILT OF JUDGEMENT THEY HAVE CAST UPON ANOTHER. NOW THEY ARE OFFENDED AT THE POSSIBILITY OF JUDGEMENT BEING CAST UPON THEM.

NO JUDGEMENT = NO OFFENSE TAKEN

"

TO ATTRACT GENUINE LOVE FROM ANOTHER,
YOU MUST GENUINELY LOVE YOURSELF. SCIENCE
PROVES THIS IN THE STUDY OF ENERGY. 'ENERGY
IS NOT A SUBSTANCE THAT CAN BE HELD, SEEN
OR FELT AS A SEPARATE ENTITY. WE CANNOT
CREATE A NEW ENERGY THAT IS NOT ALREADY
PRESENT.' TRANSLATION: THE ENERGY WE WISH
TO RECEIVE MUST ALREADY EXIST WITHIN US.

"

THE ISSUES YOU FACE, AREN'T ACTUAL ISSUES
THAT ARE OCCURRING. THE ISSUES IN YOUR
LIFE, BEGIN WITH YOUR PERCEPTION OF LIFE.

THE MESSAGE IS LOVE.

BASE EVERYTHING IN LIFE ON THAT, BEGINNING
WITH HOW YOU VIEW YOURSELF.

THE MORE WE LOVE, THE LESS EVIL CAN EXIST.

IF THE MOTIVE BEHIND YOUR WORDS ISN'T TO
UPLIFT ANOTHER, THOSE WORDS DON'T NEED
TO BE SPOKEN.

"

THE ROOT OF PREJUDICE IS FEAR. FEAR THAT YOU, YOURSELF, LACKS IN A CERTAIN AREA THAT ANOTHER EXCELS. YOU ARE NOT BETTER THAN ANOTHER PERSON BASED ON ANYTHING SUPERFICIAL, INCLUDING MONETARY STATUS, RELIGION, OR THE COLOR OF YOUR SKIN. IF YOU FEEL LIKE YOU ARE BETTER THAN OTHERS FOR ANY OF THESE REASONS, IT IS REVEALING THAT YOU PERCEIVE YOURSELF IN A VERY LOW STANDARD. FOR IT IS THIS LOW PERCEPTION OF SELF, THAT A SUPERFICIAL SUPERIORITY HAS TO BE BUILT, TO MAKE YOURSELF FEEL BETTER THAN ANOTHER. BE HONEST WITH YOURSELF. PERCEIVE YOURSELF IN A HIGHER LIGHT, SO THAT YOU CAN RISE ABOVE THE IGNORANCE PF PREJUDICE.

"

THE SMALL ACT OF REASSURING ANOTHER THAT THEY MATTER, CAN HELP THEM RELEASE INSECURITIES THEY DIDN'T EVEN KNOW THEY HAD.

BY BEING THE 'STRONG ONE' YOU ARE ALREADY SERVING YOUR PURPOSE IN THIS LIFE.

THE UPLIFTING, MOTIVATING PRESENCE YOU PROVIDE OTHERS, IS A GIFT. IT IS NOW TIME TO PROVIDE YOURSELF WITH THIS GIFT.

HANG IN THERE STRONG ONE, LIFE ISN'T MEANT TO BE A CONSTANT BATTLE, LIFE IS NOT MEANT FOR SUFFERING, LIFE IS NOT MEANT TO BE UNFAIR.

THE UNIVERSE HAS A PLAN FOR YOUR LIFE, THAT FAR EXCEEDS ANYTHING YOU CAN FATHOM.

"

WHEN YOU STAND FOR WHAT'S RIGHT, THE UNIVERSE WILL STAND FOR YOU.

THE WORDS YOU SPEAK ABOUT OTHERS, WILL BE PLACED BACK UNTO YOU

CHOOSE YOUR WORDS WISELY.

THERE'S A GRACEFUL WAY TO LEAVE TOXIC PEOPLE BEHIND. CHOOSE THAT WAY, SO AN EXAMPLE CAN BE SET ON PEACE VERSUS CONFRONTATION.

"

THERE'S AN ENERGY INSIDE OF YOU, FEELING LIKE IT'S READY TO EXPLODE. THAT'S THE REAL YOU TRYING TO BREAK FREE FROM THE LAYERS OF WHO YOU HAVE BEEN TOLD TO BE.

ITS TIME TO STOP BLAMING OTHERS FOR NOT MEETING THE EXPECTATIONS YOU HAVE OF THEM. MEET YOUR OWN SOUL FIRST, THEN, YOU WILL HAVE NO EXPECTATIONS OF OTHERS. THIS IS TRUE LOVE. THIS IS ACCEPTANCE. THIS IS PEACE, FREEDOM AND SALVATION. THIS IS GOD.

TO TRY AND FORCE ANYBODY TO ACCEPT YOU, IS A WASTED EFFORT, BECAUSE THEY CAN ONLY ACCEPT YOU AT THE LEVEL THEY ACCEPT THEMSELVES, WHICH HAS NOTHING TO DO WITH YOU.

"

THOSE WHO HAVE TAUGHT YOU THAT CRYING IS WEAK, ARE THE WEAKEST. CRYING IS A NATURAL WAY FOR THE SOUL TO CLEANSE AND HEAL ITSELF. WITHOUT TEARS, THERE WOULD BE NO RENEWAL OF LIFE. TEARS ARE TO THE HUMAN BODY, WHAT WAVES ARE TO THE OCEAN, NECESSARY FOR LIFE. THE OCEAN WITHOUT WAVES, WOULD BECOME STAGNANT AND GROSS, A PLACE WHERE LIFE COULD NOT THRIVE. THE SOUL WITHOUT TEARS, WOULD ALSO BECOME STAGNANT AND GROSS, A PLACE WHERE LIFE COULD NOT THRIVE. ALLOW YOUR TEARS TO FLOW, AND CREATE THE WAVE THAT CARRIES YOU TOWARD THE NEXT LEVEL OF YOURSELF.

“

#PEOPLELIKEUS KNOW THAT WE'RE STRONGER THAN MOST, BUT WE DON'T ALWAYS SEE THIS AS A POSITIVE. SOMETIMES WE DON'T WANT THE RESPONSIBILITY OF BEING THE STRONGEST. SOMETIMES, IT GETS TIRING BEING THE STRONG ONE, AND AT TIMES WE CRAVE BEING TAKEN CARE OF, IN THE SAME WAY WE TAKE CARE OF OTHERS.

A TITLE, POSITION, OR CAREER CANNOT SAVE YOU. WEALTH IN MONEY CANNOT SAVE YOU. ANOTHER PERSON CANNOT SAVE YOU.

DON'T WAIT FOR AN END RESULT TO BRING YOU HAPPINESS. YOU MUST REACH HAPPINESS FIRST, TO CREATE THE END RESULT YOUR SOUL CRAVES.

TO GENUINELY HELP OTHERS, YOU MUST FIRST HELP YOURSELF.

"

TO THE MEN AND WOMEN THAT SEEK TO BE LOVED, YOU SHOWER YOUR PARTNER WITH THE FINEST. THINK FOR A MOMENT, TRUE LOVE CANNOT BE BASED ON WHAT YOU PROVIDE MATERIALLY, BUT INSTEAD JUST YOUR PRESENCE AND THE LOVE YOU PROVIDE. WOULD THIS PERSON STILL BE IN LOVE WITH YOU IF YOU WERE UNABLE TO PROVIDE ANYTHING BESIDES YOURSELF? IF ALL YOU COULD AFFORD TO EAT EVERYDAY WAS OATMEAL AND BEANS, WOULD THIS PERSON STILL BE THERE, FULLY IN LOVE? IF YOU LIVED IN A SMALL HOME AND WERE UNABLE TO TAKE THEM ON VACATIONS, WOULD THEY STILL BE IN LOVE? LOVE YOURSELF FIRST, SO THAT YOU DON'T GIVE YOUR ALL TO SOMEONE WHO'S LOVING YOU FOR THEIR OWN BEST INTEREST.

LOVE, SHANNA

＂

TO THE PERSON THAT DOESN'T FEEL LOVED:

WHATEVER OCCURRENCE IN YOUR LIFE HAS BROUGHT YOU TO THE POINT OF FEELING A LACK OF LOVE AND ATTENTION, LET IT GO, AS IT NO LONGER DEFINES YOU, IT IS THE PAST, WHICH IS A NONEXISTENT TIME.

ALLOW YOURSELF TO BE HAPPY, WITHOUT CREATING REASONS FOR PEOPLE TO SHOW YOU ATTENTION. LET THE DEPRESSION GO, LET THE ILLNESS GO, BECAUSE YOU ARE MORE THAN THESE THINGS. YES, THEY WILL GET YOU ATTENTION, BUT YOU WILL THEN LACK THE HAPPINESS YOU DESERVE WHILE FOCUSING ON THEM.

ACCEPT YOURSELF, SO THE ATTENTION OF OTHERS IS NO LONGER NECESSARY.

LOVE, SHANNA

"

IF ANYONE ACCUSES YOU OF BEING 'TOO MUCH'
OF ANYTHING, IT IS BECAUSE, THEY, THEMSELVES,
ARE LACKING IN THE AREAS YOU SHINE. IT HAS
NOTHING TO DO WITH YOU, KEEP SHINING.

TRUE CHARACTER IS REVEALED, WHEN THINGS
AREN'T GOING YOUR WAY.

TRUE LOVE DOES NOT TAKE A PERSON AWAY
FROM THEMSELVES. TRUE LOVE IS NOT
SACRIFICE, IT IS ACCEPTANCE AND RESPECT FOR
INDIVIDUALITY.

"

SELF-WORTH CANNOT BE REALIZED UNTIL YOU
HAVE ADDRESSED EVERY ACTION THAT HAS
DIMINISHED IT IN THE FIRST PLACE. IT IS ONLY IN
THIS HONESTY; YOU CAN REMEMBER HOW
WORTHY YOU HAVE ALWAYS BEEN.

TRUST YOURSELF. BASE ALL OF YOUR ACTIONS
ON LOVE FOR OTHERS, BY HAVING COMPASSION
FOR THE BROKEN, HAVE COMPASSION FOR THE
EVIL, HAVE COMPASSION FOR THE ANGRY, BY
ACKNOWLEDGING WHAT A TORMENTED PLACE
THEIR MIND MUST BE. THIS WILL ENSURE THAT
YOU EVOLVE TO A HIGHER LEVEL OF YOURSELF.

UNCONDITIONAL LOVE, DOES NOT INCLUDE
LOVING AND SUPPORTING A PERSON ONLY IF
THEY FIT THE MOLD OF WHO YOU WANT THEM
TO BE.

"

THE TRUTH IS ALWAYS REVEALED.

THE UNIVERSE WILL NOT ALLOW YOUR PURE
INTENTIONS TO BE OVERCAST BY PEOPLE WHO
LACK INTEGRITY.

THEY ARE PLANTING THEIR OWN BAD SEEDS
AND WILL REAP THE HARVEST. HAVE PATIENCE
AND ALLOW DIVINE TIMING TO TAKE ITS PLACE
IN THE REAPING OF YOUR PURE HARVEST.

YOU MUST UNDERSTAND YOUR IMPORTANCE
SO THAT YOU MAY BLESS THE WORLD WITH
YOUR GIFTS AND END YOUR OWN
UNNECESSARY SUFFERING. YOUR HEART IS NOT
BIG TO BRING YOU SUFFERING, IT IS BIG TO
BRING LOVE TO ALL, THAT IS GOD, THAT IS
WHAT THE WORLD IS MISSING.

YOU ARE LOVED.

"

UNLEARN EVERYTHING YOU WERE TAUGHT, SO THAT YOU MAY REMEMBER WHO YOU WERE BORN TO BE.

VALIDATION FROM ANOTHER IS SUPERFICIAL AND CAN ONLY BE AS TRUE AS THE VALIDATION YOU HAVE FOR YOURSELF.

WE HAVE BEEN TAUGHT TO WALK BLIND, AROUND A HAMSTER WHEEL, CHASING A NON-EXISTENT FUTURE, WHILE LIVING IN A NON-EXISTENT PAST.

#PEOPLELIKEUS DESERVE BETTER, AND IT ALL STARTS WITHIN OURSELVES.

"

YOU ARE NOT A BAD PERSON. YOU CHOSE TO BE PART OF A FAMILY WITH BAD CYCLES, SO THAT YOU MAY END THESE CYCLES. STEP AWAY. STEP INTO THE POWER OF WHAT YOU CAME TO EARTH TO DO.

WE ARE THE ONES RESPONSIBLE FOR OUR CURRENT ACTIONS AND REACTIONS.

WE ARE ALSO RESPONSIBLE FOR OWNING UP TO OUR PAST ACTIONS AND PAST DECISIONS THAT HAVE CREATED OUR CURRENT REALITY.

JUST AS YOU HAVE CREATED YOUR CURRENT REALITY, YOU CAN CREATE A NEW ONE, BY MAKING NEW DECISIONS, AND TAKING NEW ACTIONS.

"...WE PROCEED ANYWAY, KNOWING THE DANGER THAT LIES AHEAD. BECAUSE WE CHOOSE TO BELIEVE WHAT WE WANT REALITY TO BE, INSTEAD OF SEEING IT FOR WHAT IT REALLY IS."

-   #PEOPLELIKEUS

"

#PEOPLELIKEUS ARE THE STRENGTH, THE VOICE, THE ONES WHO AREN'T FEARFUL OF SPEAKING TRUTH. WE HAVE BEEN GIVEN THIS STRENGTH TO USE IT IN A POSITIVE MANNER THAT CREATES CHANGE IN THE WORLD. TO HIDE YOUR VOICE IN FEAR, WOULD BE DISLOYAL TO YOUR SOUL, AND A DISSERVICE TO THE HUMAN RACE.

THE WEAKEST PEOPLE, ARE THE ONES THAT FIGHT FOR POWER.

I WAS ABLE TO SEE WHAT I REALLY THOUGHT OF MYSELF, WHEN I LISTENED TO WHAT I SAID ABOUT OTHERS.

WHAT YOU SEE IN ME, RESIDES IN YOU.

"

IS WHAT YOU'RE DOING IN LIFE, HELPING
OTHERS EVOLVE?

WHEN A PERSON BRINGS YOU SUNSHINE WITH
THEIR PRESENCE, THEY'RE USUALLY THE ONES
STANDING IN THE MIDST OF A STORM. LET THEM
KNOW THEY'RE APPRECIATED.

WHEN BOUNDARIES ARE PLACED, TRUE
INTENTIONS ARE REVEALED.

WHEN I REALIZED THAT MY WORDS ARE A
DIRECT REFLECTION OF HOW O FEEL ABOUT
MYSELF, I BEGAN TO CHOOSE MY WORDS WISER.

"

WHEN I REMEMBERED MY OWN VALUE, THE
COMFORTABILITY OF ANOTHER WAS NO
LONGER MY PRIORITY.

WHEN THINGS DON'T WORK OUT HOW YOU
EXPECTED THEM TO, BE THANKFUL. THE
UNIVERSE HAS SOMETHING BETTER IN MIND,
SOMETHING THAT INCLUDES THE EVOLUTION OF
YOUR SOUL.

WHEN YOU JUDGE PEOPLE, YOU
AUTOMATICALLY ASSUME THEY ARE JUDGING
YOU. THIS CREATES TENSION, AND ISSUES THAT
DON'T TRULY EXIST WITHOUT YOUR MENTAL
CREATION OF THEM.

"

THE ONLY WAY TO KNOW IF ANOTHER LOVES YOU GENUINELY, IS WHEN YOU ARE UNABLE TO PROVIDE ANYTHING FOR THEM.

WHEN YOU REBUILD THE FOUNDATION IN WHICH YOU EXIST, TO THAT OF LOVE, JUSTICE WILL BE SERVED TO THOSE IN YOUR LIFE THAT CONTINUE TO EXUDE NEGATIVITY TOWARDS YOU.

DON'T TAKE IT INTO YOUR OWN HANDS.

THE UNIVERSE KNOWS WHAT TO DO.

YOU HAVE ALWAYS HAD ALL OF THE ANSWERS. YOU HAVE BEEN TAUGHT NOT TO TRUST YOURSELF.

IT'S TIME TO BELIEVE IN YOURSELF, FOR IT IS THERE YOUR FREEDOM AWAITS. IT IS THERE, GOD HAS ALWAYS BEEN.

>

YOU KNOW WHAT TO DO.

"

YOU AREN'T REQUIRED TO BE WHO YOU'VE
BEEN IN THE PAST, JUST BECAUSE PEOPLE WANT
TO CONTINUE TO PERCEIVE YOU THAT WAY.

YOU ARE ALLOWED TO EVOLVE; YOU ARE
ALLOWED TO CHANGE.

HOWEVER, YOU CANNOT EVOLVE UNLESS, YOU
ALLOW OTHERS TO ALSO EVOLVE. ITS TIME TO
REMOVE THE LABELS THAT ARE SEALING THE
BOX YOU HAVE KEPT OTHERS IN, BECAUSE YOU
ARE ALSO KEEPING YOURSELF CONFINED.

WE MUST HELP EACH OTHER GROW, BY
ALLOWING ONE ANOTHER TO CHANGE.

BELIEVE IN YOUR BIGGER PICTURE.

“

YOUR HAPPINESS AFFECTS YOUR HOME, KIDS,
AND ENVIRONMENT, ALL OF WHICH ARE A
PART OF THIS EARTH.

YOUR HAPPINESS AFFECTS THE WORLD.

YOUR PAST DIDN'T HAPPEN TO LEAVE YOU WITH
A FEELING OF GUILT. YOUR PAST WAS MEANT TO
TEACH YOU, AND IN THESE EXPERIENCES,
GROWTH CAN OCCUR.

YOUR THOUGHTS ARE MANIFESTING ISSUES
THAT WOULDN'T NATURALLY EXIST WITHOUT
THEM.

"

YOUR REFUSAL TO LOOK IN THE MIRROR AND
SEE THAT YOU ARE YOUR ONLY PROBLEM, IS
WHAT WILL KEEP YOU IN THE REPEATED CYCLE
YOU'VE CALLED LIFE THUS FAR.

"

YOU HAVE NEVER GIVEN LOVE TO THE WRONG
PERSON.

EVERY PERSON YOU HAVE LOVED, HAS BEEN
PLACED IN YOUR LIFE AS A MIRROR TO SEE
WHAT NEEDS HEALING WITHIN YOURSELF.

EVOLVE

"

ALL GREAT TEACHERS, PHILOSOPHERS AND PROPHETS, HAD A SOURCE OF KNOWLEDGE BEYOND THEIR OWN. THIS IS WHAT YOU MUST SEEK, TO MAKE A DIFFERENCE.

ASCENSION:

THE ACT OF RISING TO AN IMPORTANT POSITION, OR HIGHER LEVEL.

BELIEVE IN YOURSELF.

CHOOSE TO ELEVATE YOUR MIND, BY LISTENING TO YOUR INTUITION.

"

WHETHER THE ENERGY YOU EXPEND IS PHYSICAL, MENTAL, OR EMOTIONAL, IT IS ENERGY, AND YOU MUST REPLENISH YOURSELF ALL THE SAME.

ENERGY IS MORE TANGIBLE THAN PHYSICALITY, BECAUSE IT IS WHAT WE ARE AT THE CORE.

EVOLUTION SCARES PEOPLE, IF IT IS NOT THEIR OWN.

HOWEVER, SAID PEOPLE, ALSO REFUSE TO EVOLVE.

"

WHEN YOU ALLOW YOUR ENTIRE LIFE TO BE BASED AROUND YOUR INCOME, YOU ARE ALLOWING A SPACE FOR YOUR ENTIRE LIFE TO CRUMBLE AT THE LOSS OF THAT INCOME.

WHEN YOU ALLOW YOUR ENTIRE LIFE TO BE BASED AROUND A PERSON/ PEOPLE, YOU ARE ALLOWING A SPACE FOR YOUR ENTIRE LIFE TO CRUMBLE AT THE LOSS OF THOSE PEOPLE.

"

FAITH WILL BE REQUIRED DURING THIS TIME OF
CHANGE, BECAUSE OUR MINDS CANNOT
FATHOM THE BIGGER PICTURE, THE PICTURE
THAT HAS BEEN PAINTED SINCE THE MOMENT OF
YOUR BIRTH.

IT'S OK FOR PEOPLE TO THINK YOU ARE FAKING
CHANGE.

THEY'RE SIMPLY DEMONSTRATING THEIR OWN
INABILITY TO CHANGE.

PEOPLES LACK OF CONFIDENCE IN YOU, HAS
NOTHING TO DO WITH YOU.

FAITH.

YOU ARE LOVED.

"

FEAR IS A TACTIC TO STEAL YOUR HOPE AND KEEP YOUR VIBRATION LOW. DON'T BELIEVE EVERYTHING YOU'RE TOLD, FOR IT IS YOUR THOUGHTS THAT CREATE YOUR REALITY. A FEARFUL MIND WILL CREATE HELL.

FEAR WILL NOT CHANGE THE WRONGS OF THIS WORLD, BUT MAKE THEM STRONGER.

WHEN YOU STAND UP FOR WHAT'S RIGHT, THE UNIVERSE WILL PROVIDE.

"

IN EVERY DECISION YOU MAKE, ASK YOURSELF,
IS THE MOTIVE BEHIND IT IN THE BEST INTEREST
OF ALL INVOLVED?

I HOPE TO BE AN EXAMPLE OF LIVING A FEARLESS
LIFE BASED ON LOVE AND FAITH, GUIDED BY
INTUITION.

I AM NOT HERE TO GIVE A WARM FUZZY
FEELING WITH EVERY WORD THAT I SPEAK. I AM
HERE TO AWAKEN SOMETHING INSIDE OF YOU
THAT WANTS TO COME CLEAN AND START
OVER WITH NO FEAR OR SHAME, IN THE NAME
OF CHANGE.

"

I HAD TO HAVE FAITH, BECAUSE I DIDN'T HAVE A
PLAN.

“

IF THE TRUTH DOESN'T RESONATE WITH YOU, IT
DOESN'T CHANGE IT FROM BEING THE TRUTH, IT
JUST MEANS YOU ARE NOT YET READY TO
BELIEVE IT.

"

"…IN FEAR OF BEING THE WEAKEST BEINGS TO INHABIT THIS EARTH, THEY SOUGHT CONTROL, AND WE ALLOWED THEM TO OBTAIN IT."

LOGIC HAS BEEN PLACED UPON US TO KEEP US FROM ACKNOWLEDGING THE MIRACLES THAT ARE AVAILABLE TO US NATURALLY.

LOGIC CAN EXPLAIN AWAY THE MAGIC, WHAT IT CANNOT DO IS MAKE IT UNTRUE.

WHEN PEOPLE FIND TRUE LOVE FOR THEMSELVES, THEY WILL NO LONGER REQUIRE BEING CLASSIFIED AS ANY OTHER GROUP THAN HUMAN.

"

WHEN YOU ARE DOWN TO YOUR LAST BIT OF
FAITH, LAST BIT OF HOPE, LAST BIT OF STRENGTH,
THE UNIVERSE WILL PROVE TO YOU, WHY
YOU'VE HELD ON FOR THIS LONG.

TO HAVE NO WORRY OF ANOTHER'S OPINIONS
IS TRUE FREEDOM AND IS ONE OF THE MOST
EXHILARATING MOMENTS YOU WILL
EXPERIENCE IN THIS LIFE.

BUILD YOUR FOUNDATION OF EXISTENCE TO
LOVE, IN THE ENERGY OF CREATION, YOU
CANNOT FALL. THIS IS NOT A PHYSICAL BATTLE.

“

MY MESSAGES OF TRUTH ARE NOT DELIVERED
WITH POPULARITY IN MIND, BUT RATHER,
HUMANITY AT HEART.

"

WE WERE CREATED FREE, BUT AS SOON AS WE
ARE BORN, WE ARE DIVIDED AND DEFINED BY
GENDER, RACE, RELIGION, COMMUNITY,
COUNTRY, AND NATION. IN ORDER TO BREAK
FREE FROM THIS DIVISION THAT IS NOT
NATURAL TO US, WE MUST UNDERSTAND THAT
IT HAS ALL BEEN FORMULATED FOR A GREATER
PLAN TO KEEP DIVISION ALIVE AMONGST THE
EARTH. WE MUST ACKNOWLEDGE THAT NONE
OF IT DEFINES THE EXISTENCE OF OUR SOUL.

“

OTHERS WILL CRITICIZE YOU OUT OF ANGER
THAT THEY DO NOT POSSESS THE SAME
COURAGE AS YOU.

MOVE FORWARD.

LOVE IS YOUR PHYSICAL PROTECTION, FOR IT IS
THE MOST POWERFUL ENERGY ONE CAN
POSSESS. IN LOVE, ONE WILL NOT ATTRACT
HARM, BUT IN FEAR, ONE WILL ATTRACT
EVERYTHING THEY ARE FEARFUL OF.

TO STAND UP AND STAND OUT, YOU MUST
SACRIFICE THE POPULAR VOTE.

"

REMAINING ATTACHED TO OLD PROMISES,
KEEPS YOU ATTACHED TO AN OLD TIME, AN
OLD LIFE.

TIME DOES NOT EXIST, ONLY THE PRESENT
EXISTS. IN ORDER TO GROW, YOU MUST
DETACH FROM ALL PAST RELATIONSHIPS,
PROMISES, AND EXPECTATIONS, THAT ARE NO
LONGER SERVING YOUR HIGHEST GOOD ON
YOUR PATH.

EVERYONE HAS THEIR OWN PATH, AND WE ARE
NOT OBLIGATED TO CARRY ANOTHER, ONLY
SHOW THEM THE WAY. OUR ONLY OBLIGATION
IN THIS LIFE IS OURSELVES, THAT IS HOW WE
MOVE EACH OTHER FORWARD, BY BEING AN
EXAMPLE OF IT.

"

DON'T FORGET TO LOOK BACK AND SEE HOW FAR YOU'VE ALREADY COME.

BE PROUD OF YOURSELF.

IT'S TIME TO STAND FOR WHAT'S RIGHT, INSTEAD OF WHAT'S FORCED.

YOU HAVE SUCCESSFULLY RELEASED ATTACHMENT TO AN EMOTION, A MEMORY, OR A TIME IN YOUR LIFE, WHEN YOU'RE ABLE TO REACT DIFFERENTLY TO IT WHEN THOUGHTS OF IT PRESENT ITSELF.

"

TO MAKE THE CHOICE TO CHANGE YOUR LIFE,
YOU MUST BE PREPARED TO EXPERIENCE NEW
DIMENSIONS, NEW MENTALITIES, AND NEW
REALITIES.

EVERYTHING WILL FEEL LIKE IT'S GOING BAD, IN
REALITY, IT'S JUST UNCOMFORTABLE BECAUSE
IT'S NEW.

"

THAT SPACE BETWEEN THE END OF THE OLD,
AND THE BEGINNING OF THE NEW…

ENJOY THE BEAUTY OF THE UNKNOWN IN THAT
SPACE.

THAT IS THE PRESENT, AND ALL THAT
REALISTICALLY EXISTS.

THERE IS NO 'LEVEL UP' UNTIL YOU PLACE
YOURSELF ON THE FIRST STEP OF THE STAIRCASE.

THOSE WHO LIVE IN BONDAGE, WILL BECOME
ANGERED AT THE LACK OF STRESS, FEAR AND
WORRY YOU DISPLAY.

"

THIS IS A TIME OF UPHEAVAL IN YOUR LIFE. IT SEEMS THAT EVERYTHING IS FALLING APART. IN REALITY, THE UPHEAVAL IS OF EVERYTHING THAT IS NOT MEANT TO BE A PART OF YOUR LIFE ANYMORE.

YOUR LIFE IS NOT FALLING APART. THE ILLUSIONS OF YOUR LIFE ARE FALLING AWAY, SO THE REAL YOU CAN EMERGE.

"

THE ONLY WAY TO EVOLVE, IS IN HONESTY WITH
YOURSELF AND OTHERS.

EVERYBODY'S A FAN, UNTIL THE TRUTH GETS
TOO TRUTHY.

USE YOUR TALENTS TO SERVE HUMANITY AND
BRING ILLUMINATION TO THOSE WHO SEEK IT.

YOU MUST WALK BLIND TO YOUR OWN
KNOWLEDGE, IN ORDER TO RECEIVE DIVINE
KNOWLEDGE.

“

ARE THE INTENTIONS BEHIND YOUR ACTIONS
BASED ON WHAT THEY CAN DO FOR YOU, OR
WHAT THEY CAN DO FOR THE WORLD?

WHEN THE VISION OUTGROWS YOUR
EXPECTATIONS, BELIEVE YOUR VISION. YOUR
EXPECTATIONS ARE SELF-LIMITING.

YOU CANNOT GIVE ALL CONTROL TO THE
UNIVERSE, WHILE KEEPING ALL CONTROL.

"

YOU DO NOT HAVE TO DO WHAT YOU'VE ALWAYS DONE, JUST BECAUSE YOU'VE ALWAYS DONE IT.

YOU DO NOT HAVE TO FEEL HOW YOU'VE ALWAYS FELT, JUST BECAUSE YOU'VE ALWAYS FELT IT.

YOU DO NOT HAVE TO BELIEVE WHAT YOU'VE ALWAYS BELIEVED, JUST BECAUSE YOU WERE TOLD YOU HAVE TO BELIEVE IT.

‟

YOU WILL NEVER KNOW EVERYTHING.

YOUR SOUL HAS A JOURNEY, A TIMING IN WHICH
ITS LESSONS MUST BE PRESENTED, IN ORDER
FOR TRUE EVOLUTION TO OCCUR.

CLARITY WILL BE GAINED, WHEN YOUR SOUL IS
READY TO ACCEPT TRUTH.

THEREFORE, ONE CANNOT JUDGE THE PATH OF
ANOTHER, FOR EVERY INDIVIDUAL SOUL HAS ITS
OWN TIME TO EMERGE.

THIS IS LIFE.

ENJOY.

VISIT

www.shannastar.com